Contents

What's Great About This Book

Centers are a wonderful, fun way for students to practice important skills. The 13 centers in this book are self-contained and portable. Students may work at a desk, at a table, or even on the floor. Once you've made the centers, they're ready to use any time.

What's in This Book

The teacher directions page includes how to make the center and a description of the student task

Full-color materials needed for the center

Reproducible activity sheets to practice and evaluate writing skills

Portfolio cover and a student center checklist

How to Use the Centers

The centers are intended for skill practice, not to introduce skills. It is important to model the use of each center before students do the task independently.

Questions to Consider:

- Will students select a center, or will you assign the centers?
- Will there be a specific block of time for centers, or will the centers be used throughout the day?
- Where will you place the centers for easy access by students?
- What procedure will students use when they need help with the center tasks?
- How will you track the tasks and centers completed by each student?

Making a File Folder Center

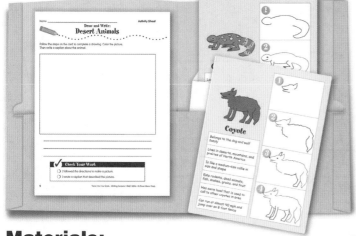

Folder centers are easily stored in a box or file crate. Students take a folder to their desks to complete the task.

Materials:

- folder with pockets
- envelopes
- marking pens and pencils
- scissors
- stapler
- two-sided tape

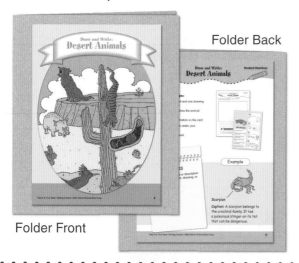

Folder Back

Folder Front

Steps to Follow:

1. Laminate the cover. Tape it to the front of the folder.

2. Laminate the student directions page. Tape it to the back of the folder.

3. Place activity sheets, writing paper, and any other supplies in the left-hand pocket.

4. Laminate the task cards. Place each set of task cards in an envelope. Place the labeled envelopes in the right-hand pocket.

5. If needed for the center, laminate the sorting mat and place it in the right-hand pocket of the folder.

6. If needed for the center, laminate and assemble the self-checking answer key pages into a booklet. Place them in the left-hand pocket of the folder.

Student Portfolio

If desired, make a writing portfolio for each student. Reproduce pages 5 and 6 for each student. Attach the cover to the front of a file folder. Attach the student center checklist to the inside front cover of the folder. Place the portfolio folders in an area accessible to both students and teacher.

Center Checklist

Student Names

Centers

Centers											
Draw and Write: Desert Animals											
If I Were…											
Make a List											
Use Your Senses											
Build a Super Sentence											
Be a Poet!											
Say It a New Way											
The Best and the Worst											
Compliment Puzzles											
Planning a Story											
Edit It!											
Science Notes											
A Thank-you Note											

My Writing Portfolio

_____

Name

Writing Centers Checklist

Name _____

Check the writing centers that you have completed.

❑ Draw and Write:
    Desert Animals

❑ If I Were...

❑ Make a List

❑ Use Your Senses

❑ Build a Super Sentence

❑ Be a Poet!

❑ Say It a New Way

❑ The Best and the Worst

❑ Compliment Puzzles

❑ Planning a Story

❑ Edit It!

❑ Science Notes

❑ A Thank-you Note

If I Were...

Task Cards

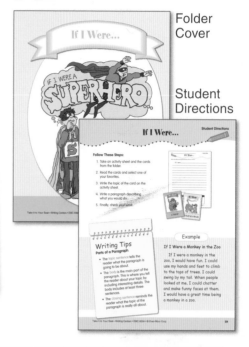

Folder Cover

Student Directions

Preparing the Center

1. Prepare a folder following the directions on page 3.

    Cover—page 27

    Student Directions—page 29

    Task Cards—pages 31–35

2. Reproduce a supply of the activity sheet on page 26.

Using the Center

1. The student selects a task card and an activity sheet from the folder.

2. Next, the student reads the card and writes a five-sentence descriptive paragraph on the topic. How to write a five-sentence paragraph is modeled in the student directions.

3. Finally, the student evaluates the writing task using the checklist on the activity sheet.

Name _____

If I Were...

Write a five-sentence paragraph describing what you would do.

If I were _____

_____

_____

_____

_____

_____

_____

_____

_____

_____

✔ **Check Your Work**

○ I wrote a topic sentence, three detail sentences, and a closing sentence.

○ I used good descriptive words.

○ I wrote complete sentences.

28

If I Were...

Follow These Steps:

1. Take an activity sheet and the cards from the folder.

2. Read the cards and select one of your favorites.

3. Write the topic of the card on the activity sheet.

4. Write a paragraph describing what you would do.

5. Finally, check your work.

Writing Tips

Parts of a Paragraph

- The topic sentence tells the reader what the paragraph is going to be about.

- The body is the main part of the paragraph. This is where you tell the reader about your topic by including interesting details. The body includes at least three sentences.

- The closing sentence reminds the reader what the topic of the paragraph is really all about.

Example

If I Were a Monkey in the Zoo

If I were a monkey in the zoo, I would have fun. I could use my hands and feet to climb to the tops of trees. I could swing by my tail. When people looked at me, I could chatter and make funny faces at them. I would have a great time being a monkey in a zoo.

If I Were

a Tomcat

If I Were

Seven Feet Tall

If I Were

as Small as a Mouse

If I Were

a Drummer
in a Band

If I Were...

If I Were...

If I Were...

If I Were...

If I Were

an Astronaut

If I Were

a Monkey in
the Zoo

If I Were

a Superhero

If I Were

the President of
the United States

If I Were...

If I Were...

If I Were...

If I Were...

If I Were

a Circus Clown

If I Were

the Fastest
Person on Earth

If I Were

an Animal Trainer

If I Were

as Strong as
an Elephant

If I Were...

If I Were...

If I Were...

If I Were...

Make a List

Task Cards

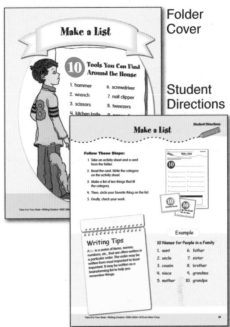

Folder Cover

Student Directions

Preparing the Center

1. Prepare a folder following the directions on page 3.

     Cover—page 39

     Student Directions—page 41

     Task Cards—pages 43–47

2. Reproduce a supply of the activity sheet on page 38.

Using the Center

1. The student selects a task card and an activity sheet.

2. The student writes the name of the category on the activity sheet.

3. Next, the student writes a list of ten things that fit the category. How to write a list is modeled in the student directions.

4. Then the student selects and circles his or her favorite item on the list.

5. Finally, the student evaluates the writing task using the checklist on the activity sheet.

6. If there is time, the student selects another card and repeats the process.

Name _____

Make a List

Write the name of the list. Write 10 things that fit the category.
Circle your favorite thing on the list.

 _____

1. _____   6. _____

2. _____   7. _____

3. _____   8. _____

4. _____   9. _____

5. _____   10. _____

✓ Check Your Work

○ I wrote ten things on the list.

○ I made sure that all ten things fit the category correctly.

○ I circled my favorite thing on the list.

Make a List

10 Tools You Can Find Around the House

1. hammer
2. wrench
3. scissors
4. kitchen knife
5. broom

6. screwdriver
7. nail clipper
8. tweezers
9. paper clip
10. spatula

Make a List

Follow These Steps:

1. Take an activity sheet and a card from the folder.

2. Read the card. Write the category on the activity sheet.

3. Make a list of ten things that fit the category.

4. Then, circle your favorite thing on the list.

5. Finally, check your work.

Writing Tips

A list is a series of items, names, numbers, etc., that are often written in a particular order. The order may be written from most important to least important. It may be written as a brainstorming list to help you remember things.

Example

10 Names for People in a Family

1. aunt	6. father
2. uncle	7. sister
3. cousin	8. brother
4. niece	9. grandma
5. mother	10. grandpa

10 Reasons to Stay Up Late

10 Names for People in a Family

10 Games to Play at Recess

10 Favorite Foods

10 Things You Could See at a Zoo

10 Things That Cost Less Than $1.00

Make a List

Make a List

Make a List

Make a List

Make a List

Make a List

10 Good Smells

10 Nice Things About Your Family

10 Uses for a Paper Plate

10 Tools You Can Find Around Your House

10 Funniest Things You Have Ever Seen

10 Things to Do on a Saturday Afternoon

Make a List

Make a List

Make a List

Make a List

Make a List

Make a List

10
Animals You Could Find on a Farm

10
Things That Are Made of Glass

10
Things to Do at the Park

10
Things That Can Fly

10
Cities in the United States

10
Tasty Desserts

Make a List

Make a List

Make a List

Make a List

Make a List

Make a List

Use Your Senses

Task Cards

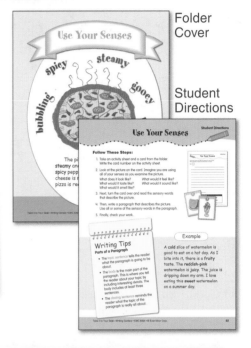

Folder Cover

Student Directions

Preparing the Center

1. Prepare a folder following the directions on page 3.

    Cover—page 51

    Student Directions—page 53

    Task Cards—pages 55–59

2. Reproduce a supply of the activity sheet on page 50.

Using the Center

1. The student selects a task card and an activity sheet and writes the card number on the activity sheet.

2. Next, the student looks at the picture and reads the sensory words on the back of the card.

3. Then the student writes a descriptive paragraph about the picture, incorporating some or all of the sensory words. How to write a five-sentence paragraph is modeled in the student directions.

4. Finally, the student evaluates the writing task using the checklist on the activity sheet.

Use Your Senses

Choose your favorite card. Write the number of the card in the box.
Write a descriptive paragraph about the picture on the card.

Card ☐

_____

_____

_____

_____

_____

_____

_____

_____

_____

_____

_____

 Check Your Work

○ I included a topic sentence, three detail sentences, and
a closing sentence.

○ I used some or all of the sensory words in the paragraph.

○ I wrote complete sentences.

Use Your Senses

spicy

steamy

gooey

bubbling

round

The pizza is ready to eat. It is **steamy** and **bubbly** hot. I love the **spicy** pepperoni on top. The **gooey** cheese is my favorite. The **round** pizza is ready to be cut into slices.

Follow These Steps:

1. Take an activity sheet and a card from the
   Write the card number on the activity shee

2. Look at the picture on the card. Imagine yo
   all of your senses as you examine the pictu

   What does it look like?   What would
   What would it taste like?   What would
   What would it smell like?

3. Next, turn the card over and read the sens
   that describe the picture.

4. Then, write a paragraph that describes the
   Use all or some of the sensory words in the

5. Finally, check your work.

Writing Tips
Parts of a Paragraph

- The topic sentence tells the reader
  what the paragraph is going to be
  about.
- The body is the main part of the
  paragraph. This is where you tell
  the reader about your topic by
  including interesting details. The
  body includes at least three
  sentences.
- The closing sentence reminds the
  reader what the topic of the
  paragraph is really all about.

cold

juicy

smacking

fruity

reddish-pink

steamy

spicy

gooey

bubbling

round

freezing

dripping

sweet

chocolaty

slippery

sloppy

warm

thick

salty

slurping

popping

exploding

burning

smoky

colorful

blaring

flashing

bumpy

fast

shiny

stinky

grimy

rotten

moldy

slimy

buzzing

bright

fresh

silky

scented

stinky

spraying

striped

bushy

black and white

fierce

fiery

blazing

green

roaring

furry

soft

purring

brown

scratching

old

brown

sagging

shaggy

neighing

Build a Super Sentence

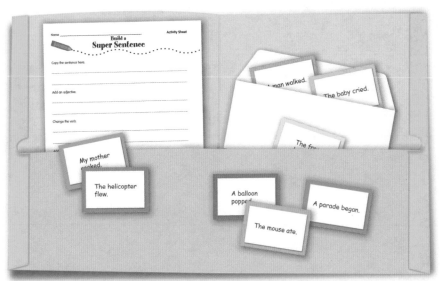

Task Cards

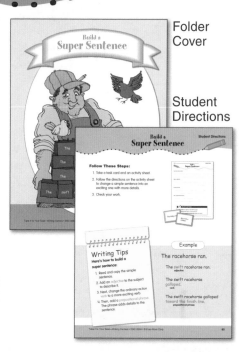

Folder Cover

Student Directions

Preparing the Center

1. Prepare a folder following the directions on page 3.

   Cover—page 63

   Student Directions—page 65

   Task Cards—pages 67 and 69

2. Reproduce a supply of the activity sheet on page 62.

Using the Center

1. The student takes a task card and an activity sheet from the folder.

2. Next, the student copies the sentence onto the activity sheet.

3. Then the student makes changes to the sentence following the directions given. How to build a super sentence is modeled in the student directions.

4. Finally, the student evaluates the writing task using the checklist on the activity sheet.

Name _____

Build a
Super Sentence

Copy the sentence here.

_____

_____

Add an adjective.

_____

_____

Change the verb.

_____

_____

Add a prepositional phrase.

_____

_____

✔ Check Your Work

○ I added an adjective to describe the subject.

○ I changed the verb to a more exciting one.

○ I added a prepositional phrase that added more details.

Build a
Super Sentence

The	racehorse	ran.	
The	**swift**	racehorse	ran.
The	swift	racehorse	**galloped.**
The	swift	racehorse	galloped	**toward the finish line.**

64

Build a
Super Sentence

Follow These Steps:

1. Take a task card and an activity sheet.

2. Follow the directions on the activity sheet to change a simple sentence into an exciting one with more details.

3. Check your work.

Writing Tips

Here's how to build a super sentence:

1. Read and copy the simple sentence.

2. Add an adjective to the subject to describe it.

3. Next, change the ordinary action verb to a more exciting verb.

4. Then, add a prepositional phrase. The phrase adds details to the sentence.

Example

The racehorse ran.

The swift racehorse ran.
adjective

The swift racehorse galloped.
verb

The swift racehorse galloped toward the finish line.
prepositional phrase

A man walked.

The baby cried.

The frog
hopped.

My mother
cooked.

The helicopter
flew.

A balloon
popped.

The mouse ate.

A parade began.

Build a
Super Sentence

Build a
Super Sentence

Build a
Super Sentence

Build a
Super Sentence

Build a
Super Sentence

Build a
Super Sentence

Build a
Super Sentence

Build a
Super Sentence

The pirate
climbed.

An alien
ship landed.

A parrot spoke.

The ship sailed.

The lion hunted.

The girl laughed.

The rain fell.

My shoelace
broke.

Build a
Super Sentence

© Evan-Moor Corp. • EMC 6004

Build a
Super Sentence

© Evan-Moor Corp. • EMC 6004

Build a
Super Sentence

© Evan-Moor Corp. • EMC 6004

Build a
Super Sentence

© Evan-Moor Corp. • EMC 6004

Build a
Super Sentence

© Evan-Moor Corp. • EMC 6004

Build a
Super Sentence

© Evan-Moor Corp. • EMC 6004

Build a
Super Sentence

© Evan-Moor Corp. • EMC 6004

Build a
Super Sentence

© Evan-Moor Corp. • EMC 6004

Be a Poet!

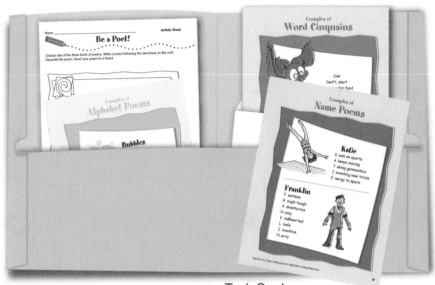

Task Cards

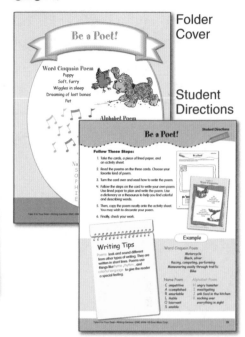

Folder Cover

Student Directions

Preparing the Center

1. Prepare a folder following the directions on page 3.

   Cover—page 73

   Student Directions—page 75

   Task Cards—pages 77–81

2. Reproduce a supply of the activity sheet on page 72. Place lined paper in the folder also.

3. Provide dictionaries and thesauruses for student reference.

Using the Center

1. The student takes the task cards and an activity sheet.

2. The student reads the poems on the cards and selects one pattern.

3. Next, the student uses the lined paper to plan and write an original poem following the pattern. The student copies the poem onto the activity sheet. How to write a specific kind of poem is modeled on the back of each card.

4. Finally, the student evaluates the writing task using the checklist on the activity sheet.

Be a Poet!

Choose one of the three kinds of poems. Write a poem following the directions on the card. Decorate the poem. Read your poem to a friend.

✔ **Check Your Work**

◯ I followed directions to write my poem.

◯ I used colorful words.

◯ I read my poem aloud to make sure that the words flowed nicely.

Be a Poet!

Word Cinquain Poem

Puppy
Soft, furry
Wiggles in sleep
Dreaming of lost bones
Pet

Alphabet Poem

Musical
Notes
Overflow
Playfully

Name Poem

Shy
Only child
Patient
Helpful
Intelligent
Eager to please

74

Be a Poet!

Follow These Steps:

1. Take the cards, a piece of lined paper, and an activity sheet.

2. Read the poems on the three cards. Choose your favorite kind of poem.

3. Turn the card over and read how to write the poem.

4. Follow the steps on the card to write your own poem. Use lined paper to plan and write the poem. Use a dictionary or a thesaurus to help you find colorful and describing words.

5. Then, copy the poem neatly onto the activity sheet. You may wish to decorate your poem.

6. Finally, check your work.

Writing Tips

Poems look and sound different from other types of writing. They are written in short lines. Poems use things like rhyme, rhythm, and colorful language to give the reader a special feeling.

Example

Word Cinquain Poem

Motorcycle
Black, silver
Racing, competing, performing
Maneuvering easily through traffic
Bike

Name Poem

C ompetitive
A ccomplished
R emarkable
L ikable
O bservant
S ensible

Alphabet Poem

H ungry hamster
I nvestigating
J unk food in the kitchen
K nocking over
everything in sight

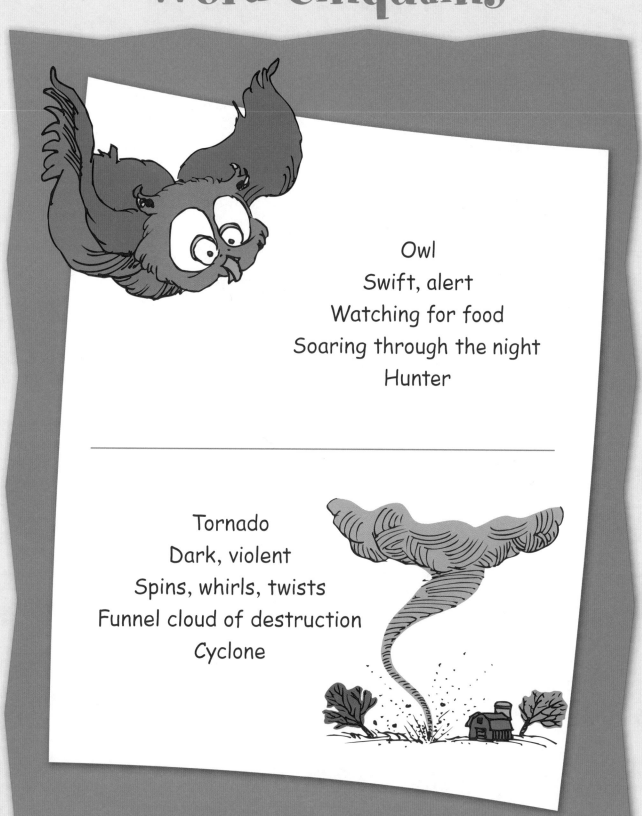

Owl
Swift, alert
Watching for food
Soaring through the night
Hunter

Tornado
Dark, violent
Spins, whirls, twists
Funnel cloud of destruction
Cyclone

Word Cinquain

A **word cinquain** has five lines.
It follows a certain pattern.

1. Choose a topic.

2. Make a list of words that describe your topic.
   Use a dictionary or a thesaurus to help you.

3. Then, follow this pattern to write your poem:

   Line one—A one-word title (noun)

   Line two—Two words that describe the
   title (adjectives)

   Line three—Three words that show the
   action of the title (verbs)

   Line four—Four words that express a feeling
   about the title (phrase)

   Line five—One word that is another word
   for the title (synonym)

Examples of
Name Poems

Katie

K een on sports

A lways moving

T aking gymnastics

I nventing new tricks

E nergy to spare

Franklin

F earless

R ough-tough

A dventurous

N oisy

K indhearted

L ively

I nventive

N ervy

Name Poem

A **name poem** uses the letters in your name.

1. Make a list of words and phrases that describe you. The words and phrases should all begin with one of the letters in your name. Use a dictionary or a thesaurus to help you.

2. Write your name vertically (down) on the paper. Make the letters stand out in a decorative way.

3. Write a word or phrase after each letter.

Bubbles

A mazing
B ubbles
C an
D ance
E verywhere

Roller Coaster

Q uivering
R oller coaster
S peeding and twisting
T hrilling the crowd

Alphabet Poem

An **alphabet poem** uses three to five
alphabet letters that come in order.

1. Choose a topic.

2. List three or more letters that come in order
   in the alphabet.

3. Make a list of words that begin with each letter.
   Use a dictionary or a thesaurus to help you.

4. Choose a word for each letter that can be
   arranged to make sense.

Say It a New Way

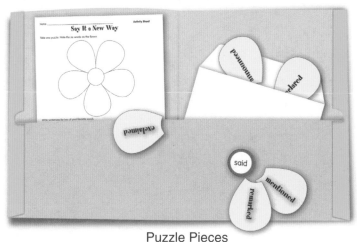

Puzzle Pieces

Folder Cover

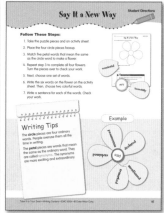

Student Directions

Preparing the Center

1. Prepare a folder following the directions on page 3.

   Cover—page 85

   Student Directions—page 87

   Puzzle Pieces—pages 89–95

2. Reproduce a supply of the activity sheet on page 84.

Using the Center

1. The student takes the puzzle pieces and an activity sheet.

2. The student takes the circular pieces (overused words), laying them faceup, and places the remaining petal-shaped pieces (synonyms) in a pile.

3. Next, the student places the correct petals around the circles to make four flowers. Overused words and synonyms are defined in the student directions. The puzzle pieces are self-checking on the back.

4. The student selects one completed puzzle and writes the words on the flower shape on the activity sheet. Then the student chooses two favorite words and writes a sentence for each one.

5. Finally, the student evaluates the writing task using the checklist on the activity sheet.

Name _____

Say It a New Way

Take one puzzle. Write the six words on the flower.

Write sentences for two of your favorite words.

1. _____

_____

2. _____

_____

✓ Check Your Work

○ I made a flower using one overused word and five synonyms.

○ I wrote a sentence for each of my favorite words.

○ I wrote complete sentences.

Say It a New Way

86

Say It a New Way

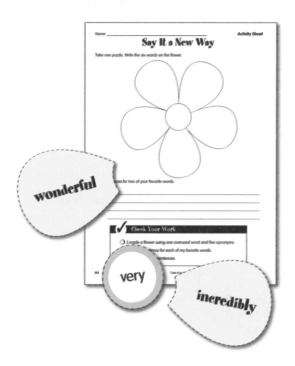

Follow These Steps:

1. Take the puzzle pieces and an activity sheet.

2. Place the four circle pieces faceup.

3. Match five petal words that mean the same as the circle word to make a flower.

4. Repeat step 3 to complete all four flowers. Turn the pieces over to check your work.

5. Next, choose one set of words.

6. Write the six words on the flower on the activity sheet. Then, choose two colorful words.

7. Write a sentence for each of the words. Check your work.

Writing Tips

The **circle** pieces are four ordinary words. People overuse them all the time in writing.

The **petal** pieces are words that mean the same as the ordinary word. They are called synonyms. The synonyms are more exciting and extraordinary.

Example

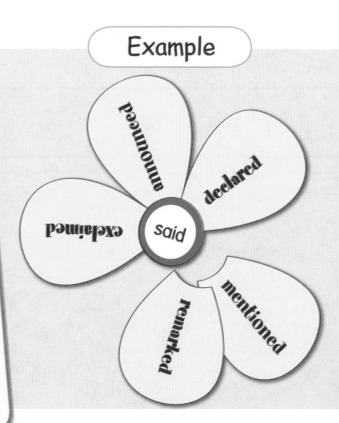

announced

declared

mentioned

remarked

said

exclaimed

**Say It
a New Way**

© Evan-Moor Corp. • EMC 6004

**Say It
a New Way**

© Evan-Moor Corp. • EMC 6004

**Say It
a New Way**

© Evan-Moor Corp. • EMC 6004

**Say It
a New Way**

© Evan-Moor Corp. • EMC 6004

**Say It
a New Way**

© Evan-Moor Corp. • EMC 6004

**Say It
a New Way**

© Evan-Moor Corp. • EMC 6004

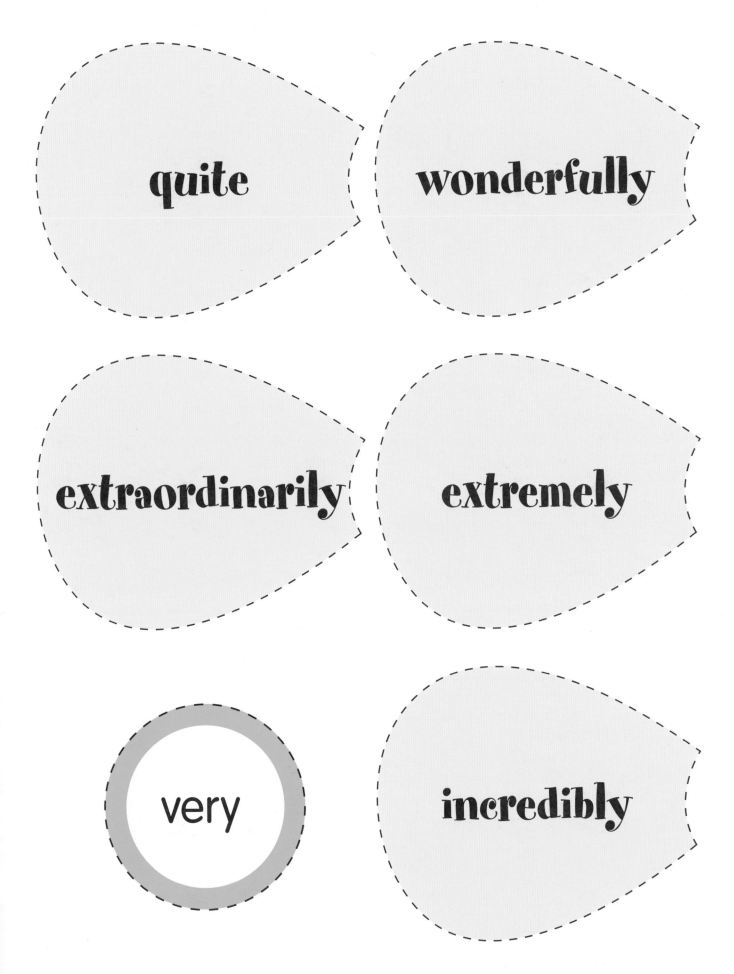

quite

wonderfully

extraordinarily

extremely

very

incredibly

**Say It
a New Way**

© Evan-Moor Corp. • EMC 6004

**Say It
a New Way**

© Evan-Moor Corp. • EMC 6004

**Say It
a New Way**

© Evan-Moor Corp. • EMC 6004

**Say It
a New Way**

© Evan-Moor Corp. • EMC 6004

**Say It
a New Way**

© Evan-Moor Corp. • EMC 6004

**Say It
a New Way**

© Evan-Moor Corp. • EMC 6004

friendly

pleasant

courteous

amiable

nice

good-natured

**Say It
a New Way**

© Evan-Moor Corp. • EMC 6004

**Say It
a New Way**

© Evan-Moor Corp. • EMC 6004

**Say It
a New Way**

© Evan-Moor Corp. • EMC 6004

**Say It
a New Way**

© Evan-Moor Corp. • EMC 6004

**Say It
a New Way**

© Evan-Moor Corp. • EMC 6004

**Say It
a New Way**

© Evan-Moor Corp. • EMC 6004

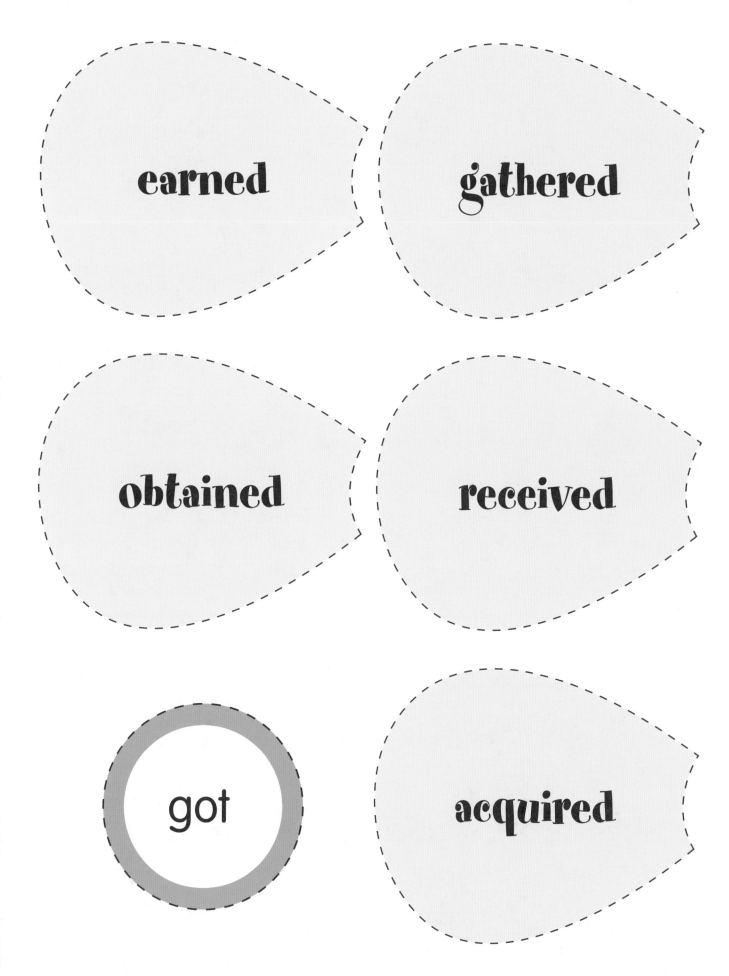

earned

gathered

obtained

received

got

acquired

Say It
a New Way

© Evan-Moor Corp. • EMC 6004

Say It
a New Way

© Evan-Moor Corp. • EMC 6004

Say It
a New Way

© Evan-Moor Corp. • EMC 6004

Say It
a New Way

© Evan-Moor Corp. • EMC 6004

Say It
a New Way

© Evan-Moor Corp. • EMC 6004

**Say It
a New Way**

© Evan-Moor Corp. • EMC 6004

The Best and the Worst

Task Cards

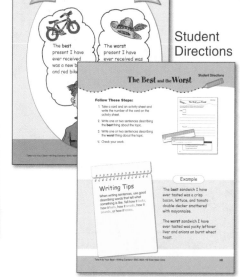

Folder Cover

Student Directions

Preparing the Center

1. Prepare a folder following the directions on page 3.

    Cover—page 99

    Student Directions—page 101

    Task Cards—pages 103 and 105

2. Reproduce a supply of the activity sheet on page 98.

Using the Center

1. The student selects a task card and an activity sheet and writes the card number on the activity sheet.

2. Next, the student writes one or two sentences about his or her best time relating to the subject on the card.

3. Then the student writes one or two sentences about his or her worst time relating to the same subject. How to write descriptive sentences is modeled in the student directions.

4. Finally, the student evaluates the writing task using the checklist on the activity sheet.

The Best and the Worst

Choose your favorite card. Write the number of the card in the box.
Copy the beginning of each sentence. Then finish the sentences.

Card [ ]

The best _____

_____

_____

_____

The worst _____

_____

_____

_____

✔ Check Your Work

○ I wrote about the best and worst things about the topic.

○ I used good describing words.

○ I wrote complete sentences.

The Best and the Worst

The **best** present I have ever received was a new black and red bike.

The **worst** present I have ever received was a goofy straw hat from my aunt.

The Best and the Worst

Follow These Steps:

1. Take a card and an activity sheet and write the number of the card on the activity sheet.

2. Write one or two sentences describing the **best** thing about the topic.

3. Write one or two sentences describing the **worst** thing about the topic.

4. Check your work.

Writing Tips

When writing sentences, use good describing words that tell what something is like. Tell how it looks, how it feels, how it smells, how it sounds, or how it tastes.

Example

The **best** sandwich I have ever tasted was a crisp bacon, lettuce, and tomato double-decker smothered with mayonnaise.

The **worst** sandwich I have ever tasted was yucky leftover liver and onions on burnt wheat toast.

1 The **best** thing I have ever tasted

The **worst** thing I have ever tasted

2 The **best** day I have ever had

The **worst** day I have ever had

3 The **best** pet I have ever owned

The **worst** pet I have ever owned

4 The **best** present I have ever received

The **worst** present I have ever received

5 The **best** sandwich I have ever tasted

The **worst** sandwich I have ever tasted

6 The **best** book I have ever read

The **worst** book I have ever read

The Best and the Worst

The Best and the Worst

The Best and the Worst

The Best and the Worst

The Best and the Worst

The Best and the Worst

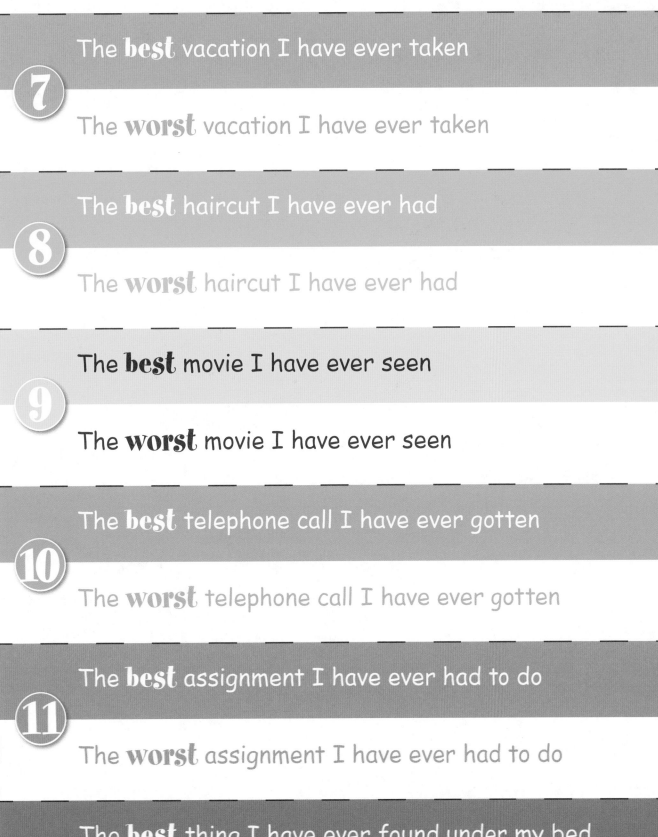

7

The **best** vacation I have ever taken

The **worst** vacation I have ever taken

8

The **best** haircut I have ever had

The **worst** haircut I have ever had

9

The **best** movie I have ever seen

The **worst** movie I have ever seen

10

The **best** telephone call I have ever gotten

The **worst** telephone call I have ever gotten

11

The **best** assignment I have ever had to do

The **worst** assignment I have ever had to do

12

The **best** thing I have ever found under my bed

The **worst** thing I have ever found under my bed

The Best and the Worst

The Best and the Worst

The Best and the Worst

The Best and the Worst

The Best and the Worst

The Best and the Worst

Compliment Puzzles

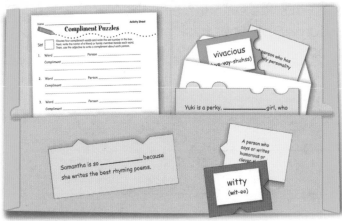

Puzzle Pieces

Folder Cover

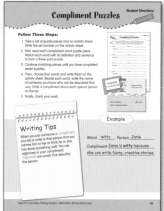

Student Directions

Preparing the Center

1. Prepare a folder following the directions on page 3.

    Cover—page 109

    Student Directions—page 111

    Puzzle Pieces—pages 113–125

2. Reproduce a supply of the activity sheet on page 108.

Using the Center

1. The student takes one set of the puzzle pieces and an activity sheet and writes the set number on the activity sheet.

2. The student matches a compliment word with its definition and sentence to make a three-part puzzle.

3. The student repeats step 2 to complete all the puzzles in the set.

4. Next, the student writes four words on the activity sheet. Beside each word, the student writes the name of someone he or she knows who can be described that way.

5. Then the student writes a compliment about each special person on the list. How to write a compliment is modeled in the student directions.

6. Finally, the student evaluates the writing task using the checklist on the activity sheet.

Compliment Puzzles

Set ☐ Choose four compliment words and write the set number in the box. Next, write the name of a friend or family member beside each word. Then, use the adjective to write a compliment about each person.

1. Word _____ Person _____

   Compliment _____

   _____

2. Word _____ Person _____

   Compliment _____

   _____

3. Word _____ Person _____

   Compliment _____

   _____

4. Word _____ Person _____

   Compliment _____

   _____

✔ Check Your Work

○ I matched four adjectives with four people I know.

○ I wrote nice compliments about the special people.

○ I wrote complete sentences.

Compliment Puzzles

Yuki is a perky ————— girl, who likes to sing and dance.

A person who has a lively personality

vivacious
(vye-vay-shuhss)

A person who says or writes humorous or clever things

witty
(wit-ee)

Compliment Puzzles

Follow These Steps:

1. Take a set of puzzle pieces and an activity sheet. Write the set number on the activity sheet.

2. First, read each compliment word puzzle piece. Match each word with its definition and sentence to form a three-part puzzle.

3. Continue matching pieces until you have completed seven puzzles.

4. Then, choose four words and write them on the activity sheet. Beside each word, write the name of someone you know who can be described that way. Write a compliment about each special person on the list.

5. Finally, check your work.

Yuki is a perky, _____ girl, who likes to sing and dance.

Writing Tips

When you pay someone a compliment, you tell or write to that person that you admire him or her or think he or she has done something well. You use adjectives in your compliment. Adjectives are words that describe the person.

Example

Word ___witty___ Person ___Janie___

Compliment ___Janie is **witty** because she can write funny, creative stories.___

dynamic
(dye-**nam**-ik)

A person who is very energetic and good at getting things done

Shanti is _____ as our class president because she never gives up.

inquisitive
(in-**kwiz**-uh-tiv)

A person who is questioning or curious

Jose is always _____ about how computers work.

Set 1

Compliment
Puzzles

© Evan-Moor Corp. • EMC 6004

Set 1

Compliment
Puzzles

© Evan-Moor Corp. • EMC 6004

Set 1

Compliment Puzzles

© Evan-Moor Corp. • EMC 6004

Set 1

Compliment
Puzzles

© Evan-Moor Corp. • EMC 6004

Set 1

Compliment
Puzzles

© Evan-Moor Corp. • EMC 6004

Set 1

Compliment Puzzles

© Evan-Moor Corp. • EMC 6004

courageous

(kuh-**ray**-jihss)

A person who is brave or fearless

Jasmine was _____ when she saved the little child.

vivacious

(vye-**vay**-shuhss)

A person who has a lively personality

Yuki is a perky, _____ girl, who likes to sing and dance.

Set 1

Compliment Puzzles

© Evan-Moor Corp. • EMC 6004

Set 1

Compliment Puzzles

© Evan-Moor Corp. • EMC 6004

Set 1

Compliment Puzzles

© Evan-Moor Corp. • EMC 6004

Set 1

Compliment Puzzles

© Evan-Moor Corp. • EMC 6004

Set 1

Compliment Puzzles

© Evan-Moor Corp. • EMC 6004

Set 1

Compliment Puzzles

© Evan-Moor Corp. • EMC 6004

optimistic
(op-tuh-**miss**-tik)

A person who believes that things will turn out successfully or for the best

Franklin is _____ that we will win the football game on Saturday.

witty
(**wit**-ee)

A person who says or writes humorous or clever things

Samantha is so _____ because she writes the best rhyming poems.

Set 1

Compliment Puzzles

© Evan-Moor Corp. • EMC 6004

Set 1

Compliment Puzzles

© Evan-Moor Corp. • EMC 6004

Set 1

Compliment Puzzles

© Evan-Moor Corp. • EMC 6004

Set 1

Compliment Puzzles

© Evan-Moor Corp. • EMC 6004

Set 1

Compliment Puzzles

© Evan-Moor Corp. • EMC 6004

Set 1

Compliment Puzzles

© Evan-Moor Corp. • EMC 6004

sympathetic
(sim-puh-**thet**-ik)

A person who is understanding and sharing of other people's troubles

Jeremy was _____ to Jason when he heard about his accident.

brawny
(**brah**-nee)

A person who is strong and muscular looking

Andrew is _____ because he exercises every day after school.

Set 1

Compliment
Puzzles

© Evan-Moor Corp. • EMC 6004

Set 1

Compliment
Puzzles

© Evan-Moor Corp. • EMC 6004

Set 1

Compliment Puzzles

© Evan-Moor Corp. • EMC 6004

Set 2

Compliment
Puzzles

© Evan-Moor Corp. • EMC 6004

Set 2

Compliment
Puzzles

© Evan-Moor Corp. • EMC 6004

Set 2

Compliment Puzzles

© Evan-Moor Corp. • EMC 6004

amiable
(ay-mee-uh-bul)

A person who is friendly and easygoing

Everyone likes to be around Mia because she is _____ and never leaves anyone out.

musical
(myoo-zuh-kuhl)

A person who is very interested in music or can play an instrument well

Theodore gets his _____ talent from his grandfather, who played the piano, too.

Set 2

Compliment Puzzles

© Evan-Moor Corp. • EMC 6004

Set 2

Compliment Puzzles

© Evan-Moor Corp. • EMC 6004

Set 2

Compliment Puzzles

© Evan-Moor Corp. • EMC 6004

Set 2

Compliment Puzzles

© Evan-Moor Corp. • EMC 6004

Set 2

Compliment Puzzles

© Evan-Moor Corp. • EMC 6004

Set 2

Compliment Puzzles

© Evan-Moor Corp. • EMC 6004

hilarious
(huh-**lair**-ee-uhss)

A person who is very funny

Chloe was _____ when she acted like a clown.

practical
(**prak**-tuh-kuhl)

A person who is sensible and shows good judgment

Maria is _____ because she saves her allowance each week.

Set 2

Compliment
Puzzles

© Evan-Moor Corp. • EMC 6004

Set 2

Compliment
Puzzles

© Evan-Moor Corp. • EMC 6004

Set 2

Compliment Puzzles

© Evan-Moor Corp. • EMC 6004

Set 2

Compliment
Puzzles

© Evan-Moor Corp. • EMC 6004

Set 2

Compliment
Puzzles

© Evan-Moor Corp. • EMC 6004

Set 2

Compliment Puzzles

© Evan-Moor Corp. • EMC 6004

considerate
(kuhn-**sid**-uh-rit)

A person who thinks about other people's needs and feelings

Jacqueline was _____ when she helped the older woman cross the street.

honorable
(**on**-ur-uh-buhl)

A person who keeps his or her promises

Paul is an _____ boy because his friends trust him with their secrets.

Set 2

Compliment Puzzles

Set 2

Compliment Puzzles

Set 2

Compliment Puzzles

Set 2

Compliment Puzzles

Set 2

Compliment Puzzles

Set 2

Compliment Puzzles

Planning a Story

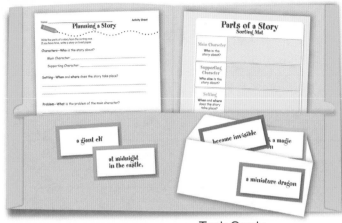

Task Cards

Folder Cover

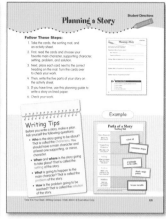

Student Directions

Preparing the Center

1. Prepare a folder following the directions on page 3.

    Cover—page 129

    Student Directions—page 131

    Sorting Mat—page 133

    Task Cards—pages 135–143

2. Reproduce a supply of the activity sheet on page 128. Place a supply of lined paper in the folder also.

Using the Center

1. The student takes an activity sheet, the task cards, and the sorting mat from the folder.

2. First, the student looks through the cards and selects one of each color— main character, supporting character, setting, problem, and solution.

3. Next, the student reads each card and places it next to the correct heading on the sorting mat. The parts of a story are defined in the student directions. The cards are self-checking on the back.

4. Then the student writes the parts of the story on the activity sheet.

5. Finally, the student evaluates the writing task using the checklist on the activity sheet.

6. If there is time, the student uses this planning sheet to write a creative story on lined paper.

Planning a Story

Write the parts of a story from the sorting mat.
If you have time, write a story on lined paper.

Characters—**Who** is the story about?

Main Character: _____

Supporting Character: _____

Setting—**When** and **where** does the story take place?

_____

_____

Problem—**What** is the problem of the main character?

_____

Solution—**How** does the problem get solved?

_____

✔ **Check Your Work**

- ○ I chose a main and a supporting character for my story.
- ○ I chose a problem.
- ○ I chose a solution.
- ○ I am ready to write my story.

Planning a Story

Planning a Story

Follow These Steps:

1. Take the cards, the sorting mat, and an activity sheet.

2. First, read the cards and choose your favorite main character, supporting character, setting, problem, and solution.

3. Next, place each card next to the correct heading on the mat. Turn the cards over to check your work.

4. Then, write the five parts of your story on the activity sheet.

5. If you have time, use this planning guide to write a story on lined paper.

6. Check your work.

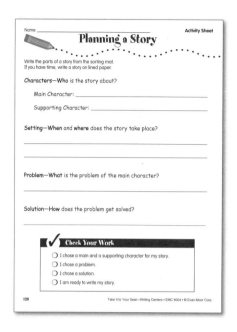

Writing Tips

Before you write a story, make a plan. Ask yourself the following questions:

- **Who** is the story going to be about? That is called the characters. You should have a main character and at least one supporting, or minor, character.

- **When** and **where** is the story going to take place? That is called the setting of the story.

- **What** is going to happen to the main character? That is called the problem of the story.

- **How** is the problem going to be resolved? That is called the solution of the story.

Example

Parts of a Story
Sorting Mat

Main Character **Who** is the story about?	
Supporting Character **Who else** is the story about?	
Setting **When** and **where** does the story take place?	
Problem **What** is the problem of the main character?	
Solution **How** does the problem get solved?	

134

a giant elf

a mischievous dog

a sickly polar bear

a timid explorer

a scared
racecar driver

a nervous
zookeeper

a kind robot

a silly surfer

Main Character (Who?)

Planning a Story

© Evan-Moor Corp. • EMC 6004

Main Character (Who?)

Planning a Story

© Evan-Moor Corp. • EMC 6004

Main Character (Who?)

Planning a Story

© Evan-Moor Corp. • EMC 6004

Main Character (Who?)

Planning a Story

© Evan-Moor Corp. • EMC 6004

Main Character (Who?)

Planning a Story

© Evan-Moor Corp. • EMC 6004

Main Character (Who?)

Planning a Story

© Evan-Moor Corp. • EMC 6004

Main Character (Who?)

Planning a Story

© Evan-Moor Corp. • EMC 6004

Main Character (Who?)

Planning a Story

© Evan-Moor Corp. • EMC 6004

a friendly alien	a miniature dragon
a cheerful drummer	a funny cook
a courteous clown	a brave baby
a gorgeous lizard	a shy tarantula

Supporting
Character (Who?)

Planning a Story

© Evan-Moor Corp. • EMC 6004

Supporting
Character (Who?)

Planning a Story

© Evan-Moor Corp. • EMC 6004

Supporting
Character (Who?)

Planning a Story

© Evan-Moor Corp. • EMC 6004

Supporting
Character (Who?)

Planning a Story

© Evan-Moor Corp. • EMC 6004

Supporting
Character (Who?)

Planning a Story

© Evan-Moor Corp. • EMC 6004

Supporting
Character (Who?)

Planning a Story

© Evan-Moor Corp. • EMC 6004

Supporting
Character (Who?)

Planning a Story

© Evan-Moor Corp. • EMC 6004

Supporting
Character (Who?)

Planning a Story

© Evan-Moor Corp. • EMC 6004

on a dark night in a secret hiding place,

during a snowstorm on a lonely country road,

on Saturday morning in Grandpa's attic,

after school in the garage,

on a moonlit night at a junkyard,

at midnight in the castle,

on a sunny day in the mountains,

after lunch at the shopping mall,

Setting
(When? Where?)

Planning a Story
© Evan-Moor Corp. • EMC 6004

Setting
(When? Where?)

Planning a Story
© Evan-Moor Corp. • EMC 6004

Setting
(When? Where?)

Planning a Story
© Evan-Moor Corp. • EMC 6004

Setting
(When? Where?)

Planning a Story
© Evan-Moor Corp. • EMC 6004

Setting
(When? Where?)

Planning a Story
© Evan-Moor Corp. • EMC 6004

Setting
(When? Where?)

Planning a Story
© Evan-Moor Corp. • EMC 6004

Setting
(When? Where?)

Planning a Story
© Evan-Moor Corp. • EMC 6004

Setting
(When? Where?)

Planning a Story
© Evan-Moor Corp. • EMC 6004

fell into a deep hole	caught a strange animal
got lost	shrunk in size
ate too much pizza	broke a window
drank a magic potion	escaped from the zoo

Problem (What?)

Planning a Story

© Evan-Moor Corp. • EMC 6004

Problem (What?)

Planning a Story

© Evan-Moor Corp. • EMC 6004

Problem (What?)

Planning a Story

© Evan-Moor Corp. • EMC 6004

Problem (What?)

Planning a Story

© Evan-Moor Corp. • EMC 6004

Problem (What?)

Planning a Story

© Evan-Moor Corp. • EMC 6004

Problem (What?)

Planning a Story

© Evan-Moor Corp. • EMC 6004

Problem (What?)

Planning a Story

© Evan-Moor Corp. • EMC 6004

Problem (What?)

Planning a Story

© Evan-Moor Corp. • EMC 6004

invented a
time machine

became invisible

found a hidden
treasure

used a rope to escape

moved to Hawaii

won first prize

lived happily
in the treehouse

left town on a jet

Solution (How?)

Planning a Story

© Evan-Moor Corp. • EMC 6004

Solution (How?)

Planning a Story

© Evan-Moor Corp. • EMC 6004

Solution (How?)

Planning a Story

© Evan-Moor Corp. • EMC 6004

Solution (How?)

Planning a Story

© Evan-Moor Corp. • EMC 6004

Solution (How?)

Planning a Story

© Evan-Moor Corp. • EMC 6004

Solution (How?)

Planning a Story

© Evan-Moor Corp. • EMC 6004

Solution (How?)

Planning a Story

© Evan-Moor Corp. • EMC 6004

Solution (How?)

Planning a Story

© Evan-Moor Corp. • EMC 6004

Edit It!

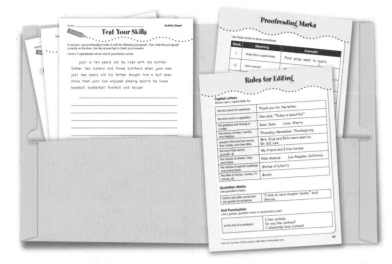

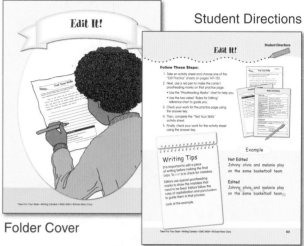

Folder Cover

Student Directions

Preparing the Center

1. Prepare a folder following the directions on page 3.

   Cover—page 151

   Student Directions—page 153

   Answer Key—pages 159–164

2. Reproduce a supply of the activity sheet on page 146 and the practice pages on pages 147–150.

3. Laminate the "Proofreading Marks" chart on page 155 for student reference. Place it in the pocket for students to use with the practice pages.

4. Laminate the "Rules for Editing" charts on pages 157 and 158. Place the two-sided chart in the pocket for students to use as reference.

5. Provide red pens for editing tasks.

Using the Center

1. The student selects one page of the editing tasks to practice and an activity sheet.

   Note: The teacher may wish to choose which language skills the student needs to practice.

2. First, the student uses the "Proofreading Marks" chart on page 155 as a guide for making the corrections on the practice page. The student also may refer to the "Rules for Editing" chart as a guide. How to edit is modeled in the student directions.

3. Next, the student uses the answer key to check his or her answers for that practice page.

4. Then the student completes the activity sheet on page 146.

5. Finally, the student uses the answer key to check his or her answers for the activity sheet.

Test Your Skills

In red pen, use proofreading marks to edit the following paragraph. Then write the paragraph correctly on the lines. Use the answer key to check your answers.

Correct 7 capitalization errors and 13 punctuation errors.

juan is ten years old he lives with his mother father two sisters and three brothers when juan was just two years old his father bought him a ball ever since then juan has enjoyed playing sports he loves baseball basketball football and soccer

_____

_____

_____

_____

_____

_____

✔ Check Your Work

○ I found 7 capitalization and 13 punctuation errors.

○ I copied the paragraph correctly.

○ I checked my work using the answer key.

Practice A

Capital Letters

=

1. abraham lincoln was the 16th president of the united states.

2. he led the nation during a terrible war.

3. lincoln helped end slavery in america.

4. i have read lincoln's famous speech.

5. the lincoln memorial is located in washington, d.c.

Practice B

Capital Letters and End Punctuation

1. have you ever visited mount rushmore in south dakota

2. it shows the faces of washington, jefferson, roosevelt, and lincoln

3. mr. gutzon borglum designed mount rushmore

4. on october 31, 1941, mount rushmore was completed

5. what an amazing sight it is to see the sculpture lit up at night

Practice C

Commas

1. On Saturday we traveled to El Paso Texas.

2. Lisa won't eat beets spinach or broccoli.

3. On October 31 2005 we had a fun Halloween party.

4. Maya ate too much cake candy and ice cream.

5. Nicki Coon is a witty smart girl.

Practice D

Apostrophes

1. The cats dish was empty.

2. All the dogs cages at the shelter were
   nice and big.

3. The childs favorite cat was in the last cage.

4. Hes a nice dog, so can we keep him?

5. Theyll make sure the animals dont have fleas.

Practice E

1. dr amanda smith is a surgeon.

2. mr and mrs alex fernandez are both principals at my school.

3. ms betty brown takes care of children in her home.

4. ms carmen rose santos is a college student.

5. capt samuel m lewis recruits young people for the Navy.

Practice F

Punctuation for Dialogue

1. This was the best birthday party ever! maya said

2. May I have chocolate cake at the party? Martin asked

3. I received two cool presents from Grandma Brown! Keisha said

4. Ben announced I got an invitation to Tom's party.

5. Angie shouted Don't eat the cake yet!

Practice G

2525 first street

seattle wa 50000

january 8 2006

dear natalie

thank you for your letter i am happy that you like
horse camp mom says i can go with you next year do
you think I could ride the palomino called thundercloud
he sounds like he is as fast as the wind

nothing much is going on here at home shawna and i
watched a movie last night i could watch <u>black beauty</u>
a zillion times

you can tell me more about camp when you get home
i miss you see you on saturday

your best friend

sophie

Edit It!

Test Your Skills

Name _____

In red pen, use proofreading marks to edit the following paragraph. T...
correctly on the lines. Use the answer key to check your answers.

Correct 7 capitalization errors and 13 punctuation errors.

juan is ten years old he lives with his f...
father two sisters and three brothers when j...
just two years old his father bought him a ball a...
since then juan has enjoyed playing sports he loves...
baseball basketball football and soccer

_____

...Your Work

...apitalization and 13 punctuation errors.

...e paragraph correctly.

...d my work using the answer key.

Take It to Your Seat—Writing Centers • EMC 60...

Edit It!

Follow These Steps:

1. Take an activity sheet and choose one of the "Edit Practice" sheets on pages 147–150.

2. Next, use a red pen to make the correct proofreading marks on that practice page.

   • Use the "Proofreading Marks" chart to help you.

   • Use the two-sided "Rules for Editing" reference chart to guide you.

3. Check your work for the practice page using the answer key.

4. Then, complete the "Test Your Skills" activity sheet.

5. Finally, check your work for the activity sheet using the answer key.

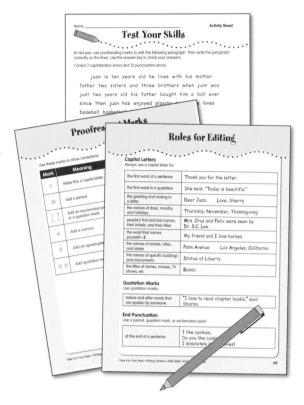

Writing Tips

It is important to edit a piece of writing before making the final copy. To edit is to check for mistakes.

Editors use special proofreading marks to show the mistakes that need to be fixed. Editors follow the rules of capitalization and punctuation to guide them in that process.

Look at the example.

Example

Not Edited
Johnny olivia and melanie play on the same basketball team

Edited
Johnny olivia and melanie play on the same basketball team

Proofreading Marks

Use these marks to show corrections.

Mark	Meaning	Example
≡	Make this a capital letter.	First prize went to maria.
⊙	Add a period.	It was late⊙
! ?	Add an exclamation point or a question mark.	Help! Can you help me?
ʌ	Add a comma.	On Monday, we will go to school.
˅	Add an apostrophe.	That's Lil's bike.
˅ ˅	Add quotation marks.	"Come in," he said.

Rules for Editing

Capital Letters
Always use a capital letter for:

the first word of a sentence	Thank you for the letter.
the first word in a quotation	She said, "Today is beautiful."
the greeting and closing in a letter	Dear Juan, Love, Sherry
the names of days, months, and holidays	Thursday, November, Thanksgiving
people's first and last names, their initials, and their titles	Mrs. Cruz and Felix were seen by Dr. S.C. Lee.
the word that names yourself—**I**	My friend and **I** love horses.
the names of streets, cities, and states	Palm Avenue Los Angeles, California
the names of specific buildings and monuments	Statue of Liberty
the titles of stories, movies, TV shows, etc.	Bambi

Quotation Marks
Use quotation marks:

before and after words that are spoken by someone	"I love to read chapter books," said Sharon.

End Punctuation
Use a period, question mark, or exclamation point:

at the end of a sentence	I like cookies. Do you like cookies? I absolutely love cookies!

Commas

Always use a comma to separate:

a city and a state	Miami, Florida
the date from the year	December 25, 2006
the greeting and closing of a letter	Dear Jane, Yours truly,
two adjectives that tell about the same noun	Nico is a clever, smart boy.

Use a comma to show a pause:

between three or more items in a series	Juan likes pizza, spaghetti, and lasagna.
between the words spoken by someone and the rest of the sentence	"I know," answered Maya.
after a short introductory phrase	After all that candy, nobody was hungry for cake.

Apostrophes

Add an apostrophe:

when there is one owner, add an apostrophe first, and then add an **s**	cat + **'s** = cat**'s** The cat**'s** dish is empty.
when there is more than one owner, add an **s** first and then an apostrophe	cat**s** + **'** = cat**s'** All the cat**s'** dishes were empty.
when you put two words together to make a contraction	he + is = he's Now he's on the table.

Edit It! Answer Key

Test Your Skills
Activity Sheet
Answer Key

juan is ten years old he lives with his mother father two sisters and three brothers when juan was just two years old his father bought him a ball ever since then juan has enjoyed playing sports he loves baseball basketball football and soccer

Juan is ten years old. He lives with his mother, father, two sisters, and three brothers. When Juan was just two years old, his father bought him a ball. Ever since then, Juan has enjoyed playing sports. He loves baseball, basketball, football, and soccer.

Edit It!
Answer Key

Practice A

Capital Letters

1. <u>a</u>braham <u>l</u>incoln was the 16th president of the <u>u</u>nited <u>s</u>tates.

2. <u>h</u>e led the nation during a terrible war.

3. <u>l</u>incoln helped end slavery in <u>a</u>merica.

4. <u>i</u> have read <u>l</u>incoln's famous speech.

5. <u>t</u>he <u>l</u>incoln <u>m</u>emorial is located in <u>w</u>ashington, <u>d</u>.<u>c</u>.

Practice B

Capital Letters and End Punctuation

1. <u>h</u>ave you ever visited <u>m</u>ount <u>r</u>ushmore in <u>s</u>outh <u>d</u>akota?

2. <u>i</u>t shows the faces of <u>w</u>ashington, <u>j</u>efferson, <u>r</u>oosevelt, and <u>l</u>incoln⊙

3. <u>m</u>r. <u>g</u>utzon <u>b</u>orglum designed <u>m</u>ount <u>r</u>ushmore⊙

4. <u>o</u>n <u>o</u>ctober 31, 1941, <u>m</u>ount <u>r</u>ushmore was completed⊙

5. <u>w</u>hat an amazing sight it is to see the sculpture lit up at night!

Edit It!
Answer Key

Practice C

1. On Saturday, we traveled to El Paso, Texas.

2. Lisa won't eat beets, spinach, or broccoli.

3. On October 31, 2005, we had a fun Halloween party.

4. Maya ate too much cake, candy, and ice cream.

5. Nicki Coon is a witty, smart girl.

Practice D

1. The cat's dish was empty.

2. All the dogs' cages at the shelter were nice and big.

3. The child's favorite cat was in the last cage.

4. He's a nice dog, so can we keep him?

5. They'll make sure the animals don't have fleas.

Edit It!
Answer Key

Practice E

Capitals and Punctuation for Names, Abbreviations, and Initials

1. dr. amanda smith is a surgeon.

2. mr. and mrs. alex fernandez are both principals at my school.

3. ms. betty brown takes care of children in her home.

4. ms. carmen rose santos is a college student.

5. capt. samuel m. lewis recruits young people for the Navy.

Practice F

Punctuation for Dialogue

1. "This was the best birthday party ever!" maya said.

2. "May I have chocolate cake at the party?" Martin asked.

3. "I received two cool presents from Grandma Brown!" Keisha said.

4. Ben announced "I got an invitation to Tom's party."

5. Angie shouted "Don't eat the cake yet!"

Edit It!
Answer Key

Practice G

Capitals and Punctuation in a Letter

2525 first street
seattle, wa 50000
january 8, 2006

dear natalie,

thank you for your letter. i am happy that you like horse camp. mom says i can go with you next year. do you think I could ride the palomino called thundercloud? he sounds like he is as fast as the wind!

nothing much is going on here at home. shawna and i watched a movie last night. i could watch black beauty a zillion times. or !

you can tell me more about camp when you get home. i miss you. or ! see you on saturday.

your best friend,
sophie

Science Notes

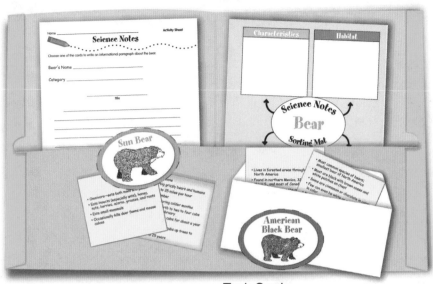

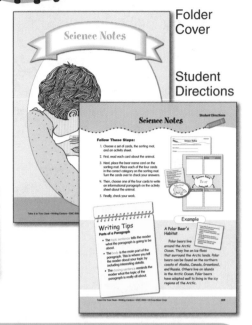

Folder Cover

Student Directions

Task Cards

Preparing the Center

1. Prepare a folder following the directions on page 3.

    Cover—page 167

    Student Directions—page 169

    Sorting Mat—page 171

    Task Cards—pages 173–179

2. Reproduce a supply of the activity sheet on page 166. Place a supply of lined paper in the folder also.

Using the Center

1. The student chooses one set of cards, the sorting mat, and an activity sheet.

2. Next, the student places the animal name card on the sorting mat. The student reads the four cards and decides in which category on the mat each card belongs. The cards are self-checking.

3. Then the student chooses one of the four cards to use to write an informational paragraph about the animal. How to write a paragraph is modeled in the student directions.

    Note: As an extension, the teacher may choose to have the student use all the cards to write a report on the animal.

4. Finally, the student evaluates the writing task using the checklist on the activity sheet.

Science Notes

Choose one of the cards to write an informational paragraph about the bear.

Bear's Name _____

Category _____

_____
title

_____

_____

_____

_____

_____

_____

_____

_____

✔ Check Your Work

○ I wrote a title.

○ I wrote a topic sentence and a closing sentence.

○ I included at least three interesting details about the bear.

○ I wrote complete sentences.

Science Notes

Science Notes

Follow These Steps:

1. Choose a set of cards, the sorting mat, and an activity sheet.

2. First, read each card about the animal.

3. Next, place the bear name card on the sorting mat. Place each of the four cards in the correct category on the sorting mat. Turn the cards over to check your answers.

4. Then, choose one of the four cards to write an informational paragraph on the activity sheet about the animal.

5. Finally, check your work.

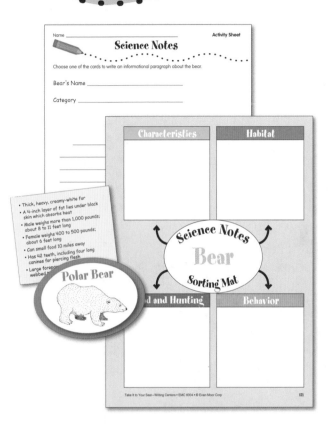

Writing Tips
Parts of a Paragraph

- The topic sentence tells the reader what the paragraph is going to be about.

- The body is the main part of the paragraph. This is where you tell the reader about your topic by including interesting details.

- The closing sentence reminds the reader what the topic of the paragraph is really all about.

Example

A Polar Bear's Habitat

- Lives along frozen shores and icy waters of Arctic Ocean
- Found mostly along northern coasts of Canada, Greenland, and Russia
- Some also found on islands in Arctic Ocean and northern coast of Alaska
- Travels on ice floes and swims between them, islands, and mainland

Polar bears live around the Arctic Ocean. They live on ice floes that surround the Arctic lands. Polar bears can be found on the northern coasts of Alaska, Canada, Greenland, and Russia. Others live on islands in the Arctic Ocean. Polar bears have adapted well to living in the icy regions of the Arctic.

170

Characteristics

Habitat

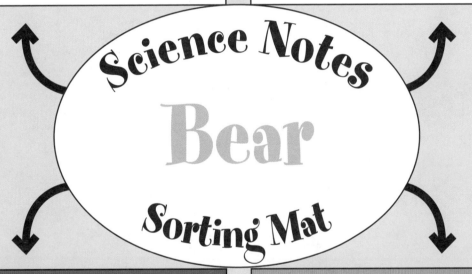

Science Notes

Bear

Sorting Mat

Food and Hunting

Behavior

- Most have a brown shaggy coat streaked with gray
- Male weighs about 500 pounds; about 8 feet long
- Female weighs about 350 pounds; about 5 feet long
- Large hump on shoulders
- Small eyes and ears; cannot see or hear well
- Keen sense of smell from moist nose on long snout
- Five-toed feet with long, sharp claws

- Mainly lives in Alaska and western Canada
- Some found in mountains of Idaho, Montana, Washington, and Wyoming
- Prefers woodlands and forests near river valleys and open, grassy areas
- Human development has caused grizzlies to select rugged mountains and remote forests
- Can survive on icy, treeless tundra

Grizzly Bear

- Omnivore; eats both plants and animals
- Roots out insects, berries, and nuts
- Takes honey from bees' nests
- Hunts mice and ground squirrels
- Catches fish in streams; likes salmon
- Strong enough to kill caribou and can outrun moose or elk
- Will feed on carrion (dead animals)

- Mostly lives alone
- Claims an area of 10 to 12 square miles for hunting ground
- Few enemies—other bears and humans
- Active at night or day
- Eats a lot in summer and fall to store fat for winter
- Rests in den during winter months
- Female usually gives birth to one or two cubs in January or February
- Lives 15 to 20 years in the wild

Habitat
Grizzly Bear
Set 1

Science Notes

© Evan-Moor Corp. • EMC 6004

Physical Characteristics
Grizzly Bear
Set 1

Science Notes

© Evan-Moor Corp. • EMC 6004

Grizzly Bear
Set 1

Science Notes

© Evan-Moor Corp. • EMC 6004

Behavior
Grizzly Bear
Set 1

Science Notes

© Evan-Moor Corp. • EMC 6004

Food and Hunting
Grizzly Bear
Set 1

Science Notes

© Evan-Moor Corp. • EMC 6004

- Thick, heavy, creamy-white fur
- A 4-inch layer of fat lies under black skin which absorbs heat
- Male weighs more than 1,000 pounds; about 8 to 11 feet long
- Female weighs 400 to 500 pounds; about 6 feet long
- Can smell food 10 miles away
- Has 42 teeth, including four long canines for piercing flesh
- Large forepaws, fur on pads, and webbed toes help it swim in cold water

- Lives along frozen shores and icy waters of Arctic Ocean
- Found mostly along northern coasts of Canada, Greenland, and Russia
- Some also found on islands in Arctic Ocean and northern coast of Alaska
- Travels on ice floes and swims between them, islands, and mainland

Polar Bear

- Prefers meat; especially ringed seal
- Surprises seal when it comes up from breathing hole in ice
- Strikes seal with powerful forepaws and claws; drags it away to eat
- Needs to eat one seal every six days to maintain body weight
- Also eats walruses, seabirds, fish, and lemmings (Arctic rodent)
- Will eat dead whales that have washed ashore

- Mostly lives alone
- Sometimes gather in groups to feed on whale carcass
- Few enemies—other bears and humans
- Can run up to 35 miles per hour
- Strong swimmer; can swim up to 60 miles without resting
- Lives in den during colder months; den is in deep snowbank
- Female usually gives birth to two cubs between November and January
- Female stays with cubs for three years
- Lives up to 33 years

Habitat
Polar Bear
Set 2

Science Notes
© Evan-Moor Corp. • EMC 6004

Physical Characteristics
Polar Bear
Set 2

Science Notes
© Evan-Moor Corp. • EMC 6004

Polar Bear
Set 2

Science Notes
© Evan-Moor Corp. • EMC 6004

Behavior
Polar Bear
Set 2

Science Notes
© Evan-Moor Corp. • EMC 6004

Food and Hunting
Polar Bear
Set 2

Science Notes
© Evan-Moor Corp. • EMC 6004

- Most common species of bears; smallest bear of North America
- Most are black with brown noses and white patches on chest
- Some are cinnamon or chocolate in color
- Few can even be white or grayish blue in color
- Male weighs from 200 to 500 pounds; about 5 feet long
- Female weighs 100 to 200 pounds; about 5 feet long
- Has strong, highly curved, short claws

- Lives in forested areas throughout North America
- Found in northern Mexico, 32 states of the U.S., and most of Canada
- About 75,000 live in the national forests of the U.S.

American Black Bear

- Omnivore—eats both meat and plants
- Eats insects (especially ants), honey, nuts, berries, acorns, grasses, and roots
- Eats small mammals
- Occasionally kills deer fawns and moose calves

- Mostly lives alone
- Enemies—big grizzly bears and humans
- Can run up to 25 miles per hour
- Excellent climber
- Lives in den during colder months
- Female gives birth to two to four cubs in January or February
- Female stays with cubs for about a year and one-half
- Mother bear sends cubs up trees to protect them
- Lives 20 to 25 years

Habitat
American Black Bear
Set 3

Science Notes

Physical Characteristics
American Black Bear
Set 3

Science Notes

American Black Bear
Set 3

Science Notes

Behavior
American Black Bear
Set 3

Science Notes

Food and Hunting
American Black Bear
Set 3

Science Notes

- Smallest species of bears
- Most have short black fur and a grayish or orange nose
- Gets its name from white or yellow mark on chest that looks like the rising sun
- Male weighs from 60 to 150 pounds; about 3 feet long
- Female weighs 50 to 100 pounds; about 3 feet long
- Has short bowed legs, and feet with hairless soles and long claws
- Has long tongue for getting at honey and insects

- Lives in dense tropical and subtropical forests of Asia
- Found in Malaysia, Cambodia, Thailand, Vietnam, Laos, Myanmar, islands of Borneo and Sumatra
- Small populations in India and Bangladesh

Sun Bear

- Omnivore—eats both meat and plants
- Eats fruit, honey, and roots
- Uses powerful jaws to open coconut shells
- Eats small rodents, lizards, birds, earthworms, and termites
- Hunts at night

- Mostly lives alone
- Sleeps and sunbathes during day
- Builds nestlike beds in tree from bent and broken branches
- Does not hibernate during winter months
- Female gives birth to one or two cubs on ground or in tree nests
- Female stays with cubs for 1 to 3 years
- Lives 20 to 25 years

Habitat
Sun Bear
Set 4

Science Notes

© Evan-Moor Corp. • EMC 6004

Physical Characteristics
Sun Bear
Set 4

Science Notes

© Evan-Moor Corp. • EMC 6004

Sun Bear
Set 4

Science Notes

©2006 by Evan-Moor Corp. • EMC 6004

Behavior
Sun Bear
Set 4

Science Notes

© Evan-Moor Corp. • EMC 6004

Food and Hunting
Sun Bear
Set 4

Science Notes

© Evan-Moor Corp. • EMC 6004

A Thank-you Note

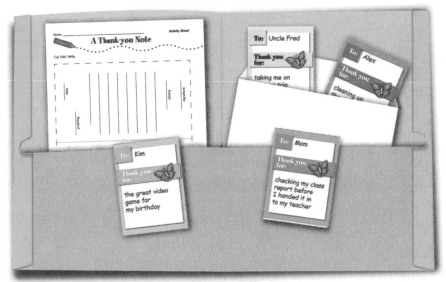

Task Cards

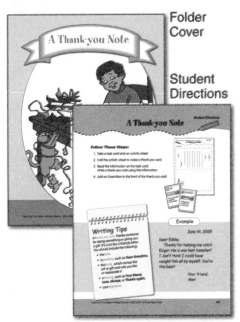

Folder Cover

Student Directions

Preparing the Center

1. Prepare a folder following the directions on page 3.

   Cover—page 183

   Student Directions—page 185

   Task Cards—pages 187–191

2. Reproduce a supply of the activity sheet on page 182.

Using the Center

1. The student selects a task card and an activity sheet.

2. Next, the student cuts out and folds the activity sheet to make a thank-you card.

3. Then the student writes an appropriate thank-you note inside the card, and illustrates the front of the card. How to write a thank-you note is modeled in the student directions.

4. Finally, the student evaluates the writing task using the checklist on the activity sheet.

A Thank-you Note

Cut. Fold. Write.

date

greeting

closing

signature

fold

Thank You

A Thank-you Note

184

A Thank-you Note

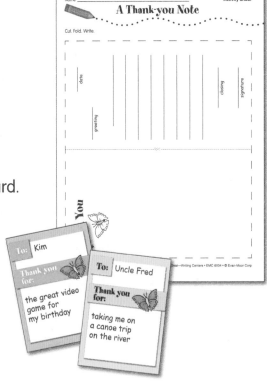

Follow These Steps:

1. Take a task card and an activity sheet.

2. Fold the activity sheet to make a thank-you card.

3. Read the information on the task card.
   Write a thank-you note using the information.

4. Add an illustration to the front of the thank-you card.

Writing Tips

A thank-you note thanks someone for doing something or giving you a gift. It's a lot like a friendly letter. You should include the following:

- the date
- a greeting such as **Dear Grandma,**
- the body, which names the act or gift and why you like or appreciate it
- a closing such as **Your friend, Love, Always,** or **Thanks again,**
- your signature

Example

June 14, 2005

Dear Eddie,
   Thanks for helping me catch Edgar. He is one fast hamster! I don't think I could have caught him all by myself. You're the best!

Your friend,
Alan

186

To: Kim

Thank you for:

the great video game for my birthday

To: Uncle Fred

Thank you for:

taking me on a canoe trip on the river

To: Alex

Thank you for:

cleaning up the mess after the beach picnic

To: Mom

Thank you for:

checking my class report before I handed it in to my teacher

A Thank-you Note

A Thank-you Note

A Thank-you Note

A Thank-you Note

To: Grandma and Grandpa

Thank you for:

the money you sent me for Christmas

To: Tommy

Thank you for:

helping me study for my test

To: Ralph

Thank you for:

helping me find my ball at the park

To: Mrs. Contreras

Thank you for:

the ride home after my bike accident

A Thank-you Note

A Thank-you Note

A Thank-you Note

A Thank-you Note

To: Angie

Thank you for:

the sleepover
Saturday night

To: Eddie

Thank you for:

catching my
hamster when
it escaped from
its cage

To: Aunt Maria

Thank you for:

taking me to the
amusement park

To: Dad

Thank you for:

helping me build
a doghouse
for Buster

A Thank-you Note

A Thank-you Note

A Thank-you Note

A Thank-you Note